Quilting

Design and make your own patchwork projects

by Barbara Kane

KLUTZ

KLUTZ is a kids' company staffed entirely by real human beings. We began our corporate life in 1977 in an office we shared with a Chevrolet Impala. Today we've outgrown our founding garage but Palo Alto, California, remains Klutz galactic headquarters. For those of you who collect corporate mission statements, here's ours:

- ◆ Create wonderful things
- ◆ Be good
- ◆ Have fun

Write Us

We would love to hear your comments regarding this or any of our books. We have many!

KLUTZ

455 Portage Avenue, Palo Alto, CA 94306
Book and components manufactured in China.

©2005 Klutz. All rights reserved.
Published by Klutz, a subsidiary of Scholastic Inc.
SCHOLASTIC and associated logos are trademarks and/or registered trademarks of Scholastic Inc.
Klutz and associated logos are trademarks and/or registered trademarks of Klutz.

Distributed in the UK by Scholastic UK Ltd.
Westfield Road, Southam,
Warwickshire, England CV47 0RA

ISBN 1-57054-215-5
4 1 5 8 5 7 0 8 8 8

Come on in!

Visit Our Website

You can check out all the stuff we make, find a nearby retailer, request a catalog, sign up for a newsletter, e-mail us or just goof off!

Introduction

Hand-sewing Basics

Design

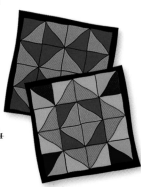

Quilting Skills and Projects

Here's what you get

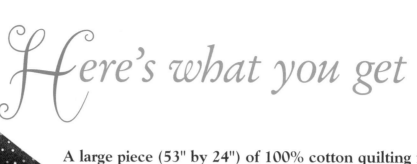

A large piece (53" by 24") of 100% cotton quilting fabric
Cut along the white dotted lines and then sew pieces
together to create your own fabulous patchwork projects.

Quilt batting
Use this to make a
quilted project.

A totally cool pressing tool
Press seams as you sew, without
needing a hot iron.

A deck of design cards
Use these colorful cards
to plan your designs.

Thread

Needles and Pins

A thimble

Small Square Template

Seam allowance templates
These make marking seam allowances super easy.

You will also need

Scissors that can cut fabric — either fabric shears or a sharp pair of large scissors

Small scissors for cutting thread

If you want to make pillows: **Pillow forms**

If you want to quilt additional projects: **Extra batting**

Planning Your Projects

The first step in any quilting project is deciding what you are going to make. We've designed the fabric that comes with this book to give you lots of choices. With a bit of planning, you'll be able to make your decision before you begin sewing and won't be disappointed by running out of fabric unexpectedly.

Each project shown in this book has been assigned a point value, depending on how much fabric it uses. (For tips on using your own fabric, see page 7.)

Important:

If you only use the fabric that comes with this book, the projects you choose need to total three points or less. Just remember…

3 points or less

If you make all 1-point projects, you have enough fabric to make three projects.

1-point projects:

Wall hanging (page 38)

Pillow (page 40)

Table mat (page 60)

Or you can make two projects —
a 1-point project and a 2-point project.

2-point project:

Shoulder bag (page 42)

Or you can make a bunch of little projects,
each less than one point.

Little projects:

Four sachets (page 34)
equal one point

One potholder (page 58)
and one sachet (page 34)
equal one point

Still deciding?
Turn the page to see a bunch of project
combinations that total EXACTLY three points.

Turn the page to see a bunch of project combinations that total EXACTLY three points.

Using Your Own Fabric

If you want to stretch the number of
projects you can make, mix in a bit of
your own fabric. For instance, if you use
your own lining fabric, the shoulder bag
becomes a 1-point project.

Once you've used up the materials
that come with this book, you can find
more in any fabric store. (See page 61
for how to make triangle squares from
scratch.) Using purchased supplies
and the skills you'll learn from this book,
you can make as many projects as you
want — even big stuff like a quilted
throw for a sofa or a full-sized bed quilt.

You'll find that the people who work in
quilting stores are ready and willing to
help you. That's their job and, besides,
they're almost always crazy about
making quilts. They'll be delighted to
help someone new to quilting. Just ask.

Project Menu

Each of these project combinations totals

exactly 3 points.

Using the fabric that comes with this book you can make any of these combinations.

You can make **12** sachets

O R

8 sachets and
1 table mat

O R

3 pillows

O R

1 pillow,
4 sachets and
1 table mat

OR

1 shoulder bag and
1 pillow

OR

1 sachet,
1 potholder,
1 table mat and
1 pillow

OR

3 potholders and
3 sachets

OR

1 shoulder bag and
1 wall hanging

My Project Plan

Project	Points

Total Points _____

Your total should be 3 points or less.

Cutting Fabric

The next step in quilting is to cut out the fabric pieces you'll need. Be sure to use good sharp scissors. It's also a good idea to wash your hands before working on a sewing project. It's easier to use scissors and to sew if your hands are clean. And, of course, you won't get your fabric dirty.

1 Start by ironing the fabric panel, using a cotton/ steam setting. If you haven't used an iron before, ask an adult to help.

2 Next lay the fabric panel on a table and smooth it out. Look closely at the markings. The dashed lines show where you should cut. These are the only lines to be cut.

3 Your cuts will be straightest if you let the fabric lie as flat as possible while you're cutting. Cut out the three long strips first, going slowly and carefully. Next cut out the three large squares. Last cut out the small squares. But don't cut them apart into triangles!

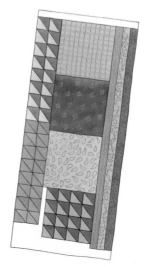

Marking Seam Lines

All of the sewing in this book uses a 1/4 inch (0.6 cm) seam allowance. (A seam allowance is the fabric between a seam and the edge of the fabric piece.) This is pretty narrow, so it's important to mark your seam lines carefully and follow these lines when you sew.

You will need:

- Small square template
- Seam allowance measure
- A ballpoint pen* or a pencil

*Try the pen first to make sure that the ink doesn't seep through to the bright side of the fabric.

On Triangle Squares

1 Lay a triangle square on a table, bright-side down.

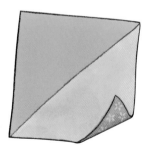

2 Center the small square template on the square of fabric. Make sure the same amount of fabric shows on all four sides.

This doesn't have to be perfect — just get it as well centered as you can.

On Other Pieces

1 Take the piece of fabric to be marked and lay it on a table, bright-side down.

2 Starting at one end, place the seam allowance measure on the edge where you want a seam line. Line the measure up so the purple seam line runs right on top of the edge of the fabric.

3 Holding the measure in place with one hand, mark a line on the fabric along the edge of the measure. When you reach the end of the measure, slide it along the fabric, line it up again and continue your line along the edge. Keep sliding and marking until you get to the end of the fabric.

Don't worry — because you are marking on the back side of the fabric (called the "wrong" side), these lines won't show on your finished piece.

3 Holding the template in place with one hand, draw a line on the fabric around all four sides of the template.

Mark all of your triangle squares this way before starting a project.

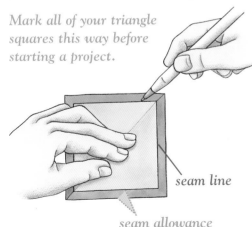

seam line

seam allowance

Using a Needle and Thread

We recommend using a double thread for all of the projects. Your needle won't become unthreaded as you sew, and your stitches will be strong.

Use the cream-colored thread for sewing seams. Save the thicker, colored thread for places where it will show.

The methods shown here for knotting the thread and finishing will anchor your sewing and keep it from coming out. Use them for all of the stitches in these projects — even the hand quilting.

Threading Your Needle

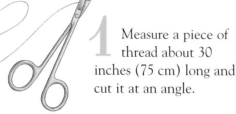

1 Measure a piece of thread about 30 inches (75 cm) long and cut it at an angle.

2 Flatten the angled end by pulling it through your thumb and first finger. It works best if you moisten your fingers first.

Knotting Your Thread

1 Thread your needle. Then hold the ends of the thread with your thumb against your index finger and loop the thread once around your fingertip — not too tight or too loose.

You'll get an idea of "just right" once you try this a few times.

Finishing

1 When you're done stitching, or when you have only about 4 inches (10 cm) of thread left, make a very small stitch.

2 Then make two more tiny stitches right beside or on top of the first one.

14

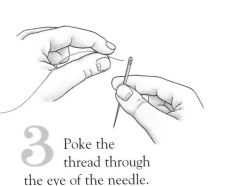

3 Poke the thread through the eye of the needle.

4 Then pull the thread through until both ends are the same length.

Tip: Hard to see the eye of the needle clearly? Put a piece of white paper on a table and hold the needle so you can see the white through the eye. Then thread the needle.

2 Bring the needle up between the loop of thread and your finger, toward your fingertip.

3 Keep holding the ends with your thumb and pull the thread all the way through, slipping the loop off your finger at the very end.

4 Pull the thread on both sides of the knot, coaxing the loop so the knot tightens near the ends of the thread.

3 Cut off the remaining thread, leaving a short tail of 1/4 inch (0.6 cm) or less.

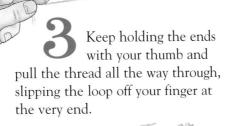

Basic Stitches

With just these three stitches, you can sew every project in this book.

You will use the running stitch most of all. If this is your first time sewing, you might want to practice this stitch on an extra piece of fabric before you get started. Your stitches might be a little bit big and uneven at first, but don't worry. They will get smaller and even out as you get going.

Running Stitch

You'll use the running stitch to sew seams that hold two pieces of fabric together.

1 Push the needle up through all layers of fabric and pull the thread through to the knot.

Hem Stitch

You'll use the hem stitch to attach a binding to the back of a quilted piece of patchwork.

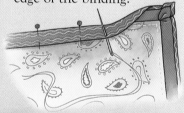

1 Push the needle up from the underside of the folded edge of the binding.

2 Pull the thread all the way through to the knot.

Whip Stitch

You'll use the whip stitch to sew two folded edges together. With this stitch, you should sew pretty close to the folded edges of the fabric.

1 Push the needle up through all of the fabric layers.

2 Now push the tip of the needle down through the layers and then back up. Without pulling the needle all the way through, make a few more stitches the same way.

3 When the needle is almost full of stitches, pull it and the thread all the way through. Don't pull too tight or the fabric will pucker.

4 Continue making stitches like this, trying to make them all about the same size.

3 Make a stitch by poking the needle through a tiny bit of the backing fabric and then back through the folded edge of the binding. Don't sew through the patchwork block.

4 Pull the thread all the way through.

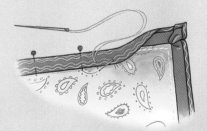

5 Continue like this, trying to make all the stitches small and about the same size.

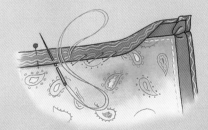

2 Bring the needle back around to the underside of the project and push it back up through all layers of fabric, just like you did the first time.

3 Continue sewing like this, trying to keep all the stitches about the same size. The stitches will wrap over the edges of the pieces you're sewing together.

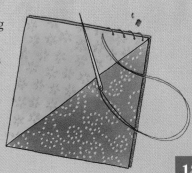

Pinning Seams

If you pin your seams carefully before sewing them, you'll get everything lined up right. These steps show how to pin together two squares in a patchwork block. For other seams, the pins can be placed about 2 inches (5 cm) apart.

1 Place the two squares bright-sides together and line up the edges where you are going to sew. Make sure you've marked seam lines (see page 12) before you start pinning.

2 On the sewing edge, put pins in the two outside corners, pinning through the corner of the seam line. Make sure you pin through both squares, too.

3 Place a pin about halfway between the corner pins.

Pressing Seams

It's a good idea to press seams right after you sew them. It only takes a few seconds with the cool pressing tool that comes with this book.

This page shows how to press a strip of squares, but the directions are the same for any seam you want to press.

Tip: Try not to stretch or pull the fabric, which could make it change shape.

1 Lay the strip to be pressed on a table, bright-side down. This way, you'll first presss the seam allowances from the "wrong" side of the fabric.

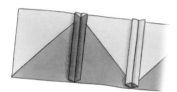

2 Hold the pressing tool with your index finger pushing down on the indented circle. Starting with the first seam, fold both seam allowances to one side and use the wide end of the tool to crease the fabric along the folds. Use short, firm strokes, sliding the tool toward yourself.

3 Repeat step 2 for the other seams in the strip, pressing all of the seam allowances to the same side.

4 Now turn the strip over, bright-side up. Make sure each seam is lying flat and use the pressing tool to press each one from the bright side.

Patchwork Design

Some folks think the best part of quilting is dreaming up a design and picking out fabulous fabrics to make it a reality.

This book comes with a unique piece of fabric that makes it easy to create your own designs — it includes three sets of coordinating prints for the patchwork itself and additional parts for borders, backings, linings and whatnot.

The Magic of Triangles

What's really special about the fabric are the 48 triangle squares. Designing with triangle squares is much more exciting than designing with plain squares.

If you have four plain squares in green and violet, there are only six ways you can arrange them…

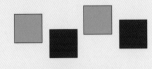

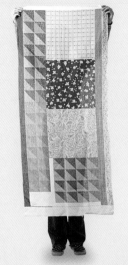

Stripes

or Checks

But, if you have four triangle squares in green and violet, there are…

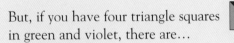

256 different ways to arrange them!

Really! You can find all 256 along the borders of pages 20–23. And to make a 16-square patchwork block, you will need to put together four of these arrangements. Explore the possibilities with the Triangle Twirling game on page 24.

Making up a Design

1 The first thing to do is to come up with a patchwork pattern. Depending on the project you choose to make, you may need a 4-square, 9-square or 16-square pattern. Any of the following techniques will start you on your way.

◆ Use the design cards (the sides with only two triangles) to lay out your own pattern ideas.

◆ Play Triangle Twirling, the design–card game on page 24. It's fun and will give you a glimpse of the huge number of designs that are possible.

◆ Play around with the fabric triangle squares until you have a design you love.

◆ Check out the 16-square patterns on the design cards and on the inside front and back covers of this book. They can be used as is or simplified to make patterns with less squares.

2 Pick your colors. You can use triangle squares from one, two or all three color combinations in one project.

◆ Using just one color combination will make the pattern created by the triangles the design focus.

◆ Blending two color combinations will add some extra zing to the design.

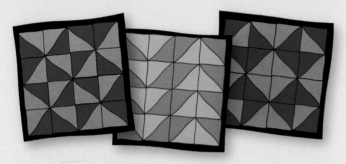

◆ Mixing all three color combinations can give your pattern a bouncy feeling or a harmonious look, depending on how you mix it up.

If you use all three color combinations in one project, you will probably need to use all three in all of your projects. Think this through before you start your project.

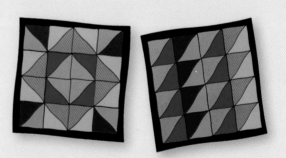

3 Once you've designed your pattern and chosen your colors, lay out the fabric squares exactly the way you want them to look in your finished project.

If you arrange your design on a tray or a cookie sheet (be sure it's a really clean one), you can put it aside easily when you aren't working on it.

Triangle Twirling

Here's a game you can play to design a 16-square pattern. It's a fun way to come up with a design, and it also gives you a hint at the huge range of patchwork patterns that are possible when you are using triangle squares.

You will need:
- Deck of design cards
- Large square template
- Scratch paper
- 4 pennies

Setting Up

1 On scratch paper, use the large square template to trace three squares. Cut them out.

2 Find all 16 design cards in any one color combination. Spread the 16 cards on a table (the sides with only two triangles should be up) and mix them around. Then gather the cards back into a pile.

Twirling

6 Arrange the groups of four to make a large square, turning each group so that the penny is in the outer corner of the square. This will often give you a traditional quilt design.

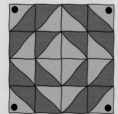

7 Now turn the groups so that they form another large square, but this time with the four pennies meeting in the middle. This is also likely to be a traditional-looking design.

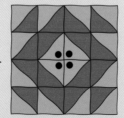

8 For a different kind of design, move the groups so the penny is in the same location in each of the small squares. Here the penny is in the upper left corner of each group.

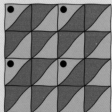

3 Place the large square template on the table in front of you. Take the top card and, without rotating it, put it in space 1.

4 Put the next card in space 2. Again, don't rotate the card, let it land at random. Do the same with the next two cards, putting them in spaces 3 and 4 without planning how they'll land.

You've made a completely random 4-square pattern.

5 Now arrange the other 12 cards on the three paper squares so they match your first 4-square pattern. Place a penny in the upper right corner of each square.

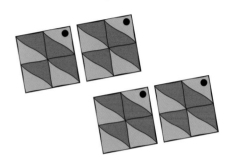

9 Make more patterns by mixing up the arrangement of the four groupings. For example, have the penny point to the middle in two opposite squares, and toward the outer corners in the other two squares.

Wow! And all of these designs are coming from just one of the 256 different ways to arrange four triangle squares.

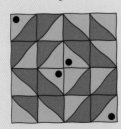

10 If you haven't found a pattern you like, repeat steps 2–9.

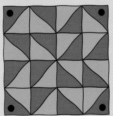 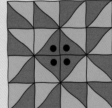 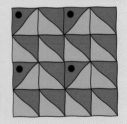

Keep twirling until you find a design that you love.

Patchwork Block

A patchwork block is the heart of any project you make. Depending on your project, your block will use 4, 9 or 16 squares. The block here uses 16 squares, but the steps are the same for the other sizes.

Before you begin, make sure you've marked seam lines on the triangle squares (see page 16).

Keeping Your Squares Where You Want Them

1 Cut out four numbered flowers (1–4) from the sheet you'll find in the box. You can cut them into squares or flower shapes.

2 Pin to the square at the top left corner of your patchwork block.

Leave the flowers pinned on until your entire patchwork block is sewn together. They will remind you which end of each strip is the top and which strip goes where.

3 One at a time, pin numbered flowers on the other squares along the top row. Now you have Strip 1, Strip 2, Strip 3 and Strip 4.

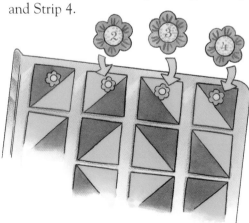

Stitching Your Squares into Strips

1 Starting with the top two squares in Strip 1, flip the second square up and over, onto the top square. The top edge of the second square (shown by the stars) should be lying along the bottom edge of the first square (the one with the numbered flower). The two squares should be bright-sides-together.

2 Follow the directions on page 18 to pin the two squares together along the bottom edge (shown by the stars). Use a running stitch to sew the two edges together, removing the pins as you go. End with three little stitches. Then flip the second square back down.

3 Now flip the third square in Strip 1 up and over, onto the second square, bright-sides together. Pin and sew along the bottom edge (shown by the stars). You will be sewing the top edge of the third square to the bottom edge of the second square. Then flip the third square back down.

4 Flip up the fourth square in Strip 1 and sew it onto the square above. This time you will be sewing the top edge of the fourth square to the bottom edge of the third square. When you're done, flip the fourth square back down.

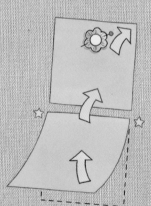

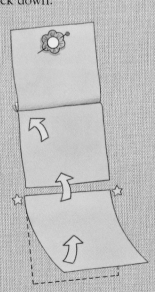

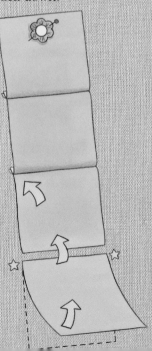

To keep things clear, we've left the triangles off the squares on these two pages.

5 Turn the strip over so the bright side is down. Use your pressing tool to press each double seam allowance toward the top of the strip (see page 19).

6 Repeat steps 1–5 to complete Strips 2, 3 and 4. For Strip 2 press the seam allowances to the bottom, for Strip 3 press them to the top and for Strip 4 press them to the bottom.

7 Put the completed strips back in their places. Leave the numbered flowers in place for now.

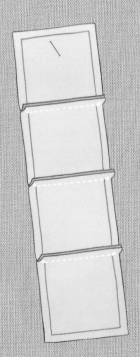

Stitching Your Strips into a Block

1 Starting with the first two strips, flip Strip 2 to the left, onto Strip 1. The left edge of Strip 2 (shown by the stars) should now be lying along the right edge of Strip 1. The bright sides should be together.

2 Rotate the strips so the starred edges are at the top. Pin the edges together, beginning with pins at each seam. Don't worry if the corners don't meet — your patchwork design will look fine anyway.

3 Use a running stitch to sew the two strips together, removing the pins as you go. Sew right through the seam allowances (one seam allowance should already be pressed to the right and the other to the left). End with three little stitches.

4 Unfold the strips so you see the bright sides again. Rotate the piece so the flowers are at the top.

5 Flip the strips over (bright-side down) and use the pressing tool to press the seam allowances to one side — it doesn't matter which way. Don't worry if they don't stay pressed very well.

6 Repeat steps 1–5 for Strips 3 and 4: Sew the left edge of Strip 3 to the right edge of Strip 2 and then the left edge of Strip 4 to the right edge of Strip 3.

7 Now take off the numbered flowers and press your block with an iron, using a cotton/steam setting. Iron the wrong side first, and then the bright side.

# Adding a Backing

If you're making a sachet, wall hanging or pillow, your patchwork block will need a backing. A backing for a sachet is shown here, but the steps are the same for a wall hanging or a pillow.

1 Choose a large fabric square — this will be your backing. Lay it on a table, bright-side up. Lay your patchwork block on top of it, bright-side down, lining the block up with one corner of the backing. Hold it in place with a few pins.

2 Carefully cut away the extra backing fabric so the backing piece is the same size as your patchwork block.

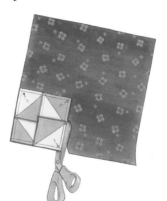

3 Pin the two pieces together on three sides, leaving the fourth side open. Then use a running stitch to sew the pinned sides together along the seam lines on the patchwork block. End with three little stitches.

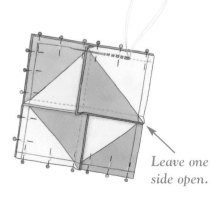

Leave one side open.

4 Reach inside the opening and turn the piece bright-side out. Use the pressing tool to gently poke the corners from the inside until they are turned all the way out.

5 Along the side that is still open, fold the edges in and crease them with the pressing tool. Now iron both sides using a cotton/steam setting.

Sachet

A sachet is a tiny, perfumed pillow that can be tucked in a drawer or hung in your closet. It's a quick, simple project — great for first-time quilters.

You will need:

- A sewn 4-square patchwork block
- A large fabric square
- Cotton balls or pillow stuffing
- Cologne
- Potpourri or dried lavender (optional)
- Ribbon, pompom or button (optional)

1 Choose the large fabric square you want to use for your sachet's backing. Follow the steps on pages 32–33 to add it to your patchwork block. Once the sachet cover is turned bright-side out, remember to fold in and crease the edges along the open side before you iron it.

2 Put a few drops of cologne on some cotton balls or pillow stuffing and, if you want to, mix in some potpourri or dried lavender. Put the cotton balls inside the sachet cover.

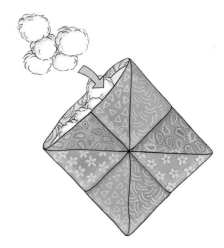

Finishing Touches

You can finish your sachet by making a few small running stitches on top of each other in the very center of the sachet.

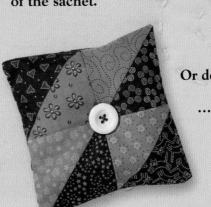

3 Pin and sew the sachet closed using a whip stitch (see page 16) and colored thread that matches the fabric. Start by hiding your knot under a folded edge, and end with three little stitches.

Or decorate the sachet by...

...adding a fancy button.

...sewing a tiny bow in the center.

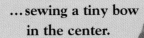

...gluing on a pompom.

Adding a Border

A border will set off your patchwork the same way a frame sets off a photo. Here are the steps for adding a border to a 16-square patchwork block — but the instructions will work for a block of any size.

1 Choose a long fabric strip to use as your border. Mark a seam line on the wrong side, along both long edges of the strip (see page 12).

2 Place your patchwork block, bright-side up, on a table. Pin one edge of the border strip along any one edge of the block, bright-sides together, and trim off the extra length. Do the same on the opposite edge.

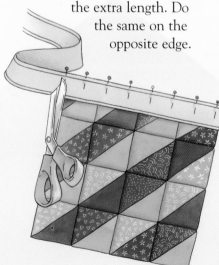

3 Sew along the seam lines, using running stitches and removing the pins as you go. End with three little stitches.

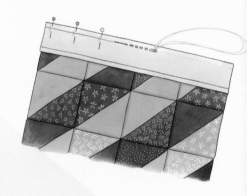

4 Turn your patchwork block over and flip the two borders out. Use your pressing tool to press the seam allowances toward the borders. Then turn your block over again and press the seams from the bright side.

5 Repeat steps 2–3 to pin and sew the border fabric to the other two edges of the block. This time the border pieces will go all the way out to the outer edges of the first pair of border pieces.

6 Press these two borders as you did with the first pair in step 4.

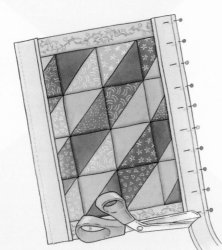

Look at the illustration carefully before trimming off the extra length.

37

Wall Hanging

Treat your patchwork like the fine art that it is and display it for all to admire. You can also use this piece on a bedside table or make a longer piece for a dresser. The wall hanging shown here uses a 16-square block, but the instructions will work for a block of any size.

1 Place a patchwork block on a table, bright-side up, and follow the steps on pages 36–37 to add a border.

2 Next choose a large fabric square — this will be your backing. Place it on the table, bright-side up, and follow the steps on pages 32–33 to add a backing. The backing should extend to the outer edges of the border on all four sides. Make sure to sew the three sides together along the seam lines on the *border pieces* (not the patchwork block).

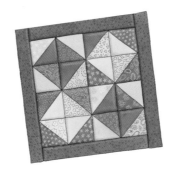

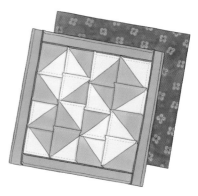

3 Make sure that the edges on the open end are still folded in. Then pin and sew the opening closed using a whip stitch (see page 16). Choose a colored thread that matches the border. Start by hiding your knot under a folded edge, and end with three little stitches.

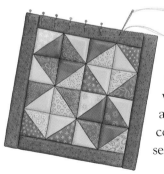

When you're done, press your wall hanging with an iron, using a cotton/steam setting.

If you ever get tired of your wall hanging, it's easy to turn it into a pillow — just remove the whip stitches and follow the steps on page 40 for stuffing a pillow.

Pillow

If you've already made a wall hanging, making a pillow will seem very familiar. The steps are the same until it comes time to add the stuffing.

The pillow shown here uses a 16-square patchwork block, which takes a 12″ by 12″ pillow form, but the instructions will work for a block of any size. You can buy pillow forms at most fabric stores or stuff your pillow with fiberfill, cotton balls, batting... anything huggable will do.

You will need:
- A sewn patchwork block
- A large fabric square
- A long fabric strip
- A pillow form or other pillow stuffing

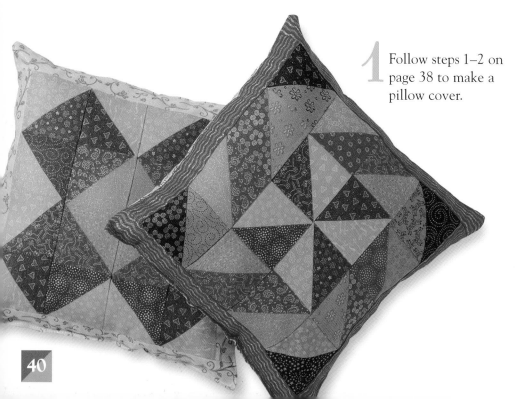

1 Follow steps 1–2 on page 38 to make a pillow cover.

2 Once the pillow cover is turned bright-side out and ironed, gently push the pillow form or other stuffing into the opening, tugging at it gently until the corners are well stuffed.

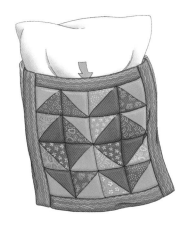

3 Squash the pillow down a little so you can work freely with the opening. Make sure that the edges on the open end are still folded in. Then pin and sew the opening closed using a whip stitch (see page 16). Choose a colored thread that matches the fabric. Start by hiding your knot under a folded edge, and end with three little stitches.

Tweak the pillow a little until the stuffing is just right. Sweet dreams!

Shoulder Bag

This is a totally great tote — and a great way to show your patchwork to friends. Best of all, it goes together in a flash!

The bag shown here uses two 16-square patchwork blocks, but the steps are the same if you want to make a mini-bag using two 9-square blocks.

Cutting

1 To cut a lining piece for your bag, lay a large fabric square on a table. Then lay a patchwork block on top. Match the edges at one corner and hold it in place with pins. Cut away the extra fabric on the two other sides. Remove the pins when you're done.

Repeat this step with the other fabric square.

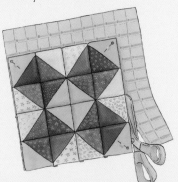

2 To cut a border and shoulder strap for your bag, lay a long fabric strip along an edge of a patchwork block. Cutting only one end of the strip, trim it so it's the same length as the block. Repeat this step with the other strip.

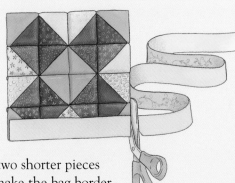

The two shorter pieces will make the bag border. The two longer pieces will make the shoulder strap.

Marking

1 On each lining piece, mark a seam line (see page 12) on the wrong side, along all four edges.

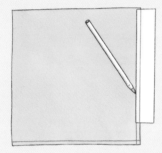

2 On each border piece, mark a seam line on the wrong side, along all four edges.

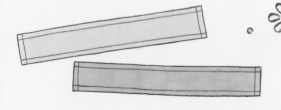

Want to save fabric so you can make more projects?

You can make this bag using your own fabric for the lining pieces and one side of the strap. Then you could use just one patchwork block for the front of the bag, one large fabric square for the back and one long strip for the strap and border. Made this way, the shoulder bag would be just a 1-point project!

Sewing the Bag

1 Pin and sew a border piece to one edge of a patchwork block, bright-sides together, along the seam line. Make sure the entire border piece overlaps the block and you sew the outer edge. Use a running stitch and remove the pins as you go. End with three little stitches.

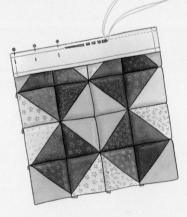

2 Pin and sew a lining piece to the other side of the border piece, bright-sides together, along the seam line.

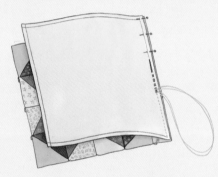

3 Use the pressing tool to press both seam allowances toward the border strip, first on the wrong side and then on the bright side.

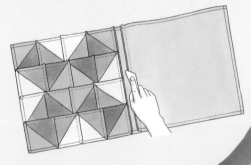

4 Repeat steps 1–3 with the other patchwork block, border piece and lining piece.

5 Lay one of the sewn pieces, bright-side up, on the table. Place the other one on top, bright-sides together. Be sure to have both blocks at the same end.

6 Pin and sew along three of the four edges, leaving open the short edge where the lining pieces come together. Using a running stitch, sew right through the seam allowances, removing the pins as you go. End with three little stitches.

Leave this edge open.

7 Turn the entire piece bright-side out. Then use the pressing tool to carefully poke the corners until they are nice and square. Use your fingers to smooth out the seams on the edges of the bag.

8 Along the side that is still open, fold the edges in, along the marked seam lines. Pin the edges together and then sew them closed with small whip stitches (see page 16).

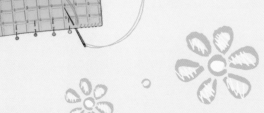

9 Take hold of the lining pieces and push them down into the bag, between the patchwork blocks. The border pieces will fold over to make the top edge of the bag.

10 Use the pressing tool again to poke out the corners, making sure that the lining corners settle into the patchwork corners. Smooth out the border pieces to make a flat band around the opening of the bag.

This is a good time to iron your bag. Use a cotton/steam setting.

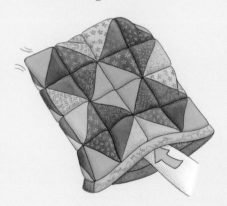

Adding the Strap

←——— 28" ———→

1 From the short shoulder strap pieces you cut earlier, cut two 28-inch (70 cm) pieces. (Save the remaining scraps for another project.)

2 On one of the pieces, mark seam lines on the wrong side, along both long edges and one short edge (see page 12).

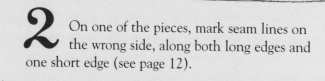

3 Lay the unmarked strip on a table, bright-side up. Place the other strip on top, bright-sides together. Pin the three sides together along the seam lines and sew them together using running stitches, removing the pins as you go. End with three little stitches.

You now have a long tube, open at one end.
The next step is to turn it bright-side out.

4 Push the closed end into the tube. Use the
wide end of the pressing tool to carefully push
the tube end in as far as you can. Keep pushing until the entire pressing tool is inside the tube.

5 With one hand, hold on to the narrow end
of the tool and the fabric covering it. With
your other hand, grasp the tube 10–12 inches
(25–30 cm) away.

6 Push the pressing tool farther into the
tube, scrunching up the fabric, until your
other hand can grasp the wide end of the tool.
Then let go of the narrow end and smooth out
the scrunches of fabric.

7 Repeat steps 5–6, moving the pressing tool through the tube, until the closed end of the tube comes out the other end.

8 Now grasp the closed end and use your other hand to slide down the rest of the fabric until the tube is completely bright-side-out. Presto!

9 Use the pressing tool to make the corners square and the edges straight. Then remove the tool.

10 At the open end of the tube, fold in about 1/4 inch (0.6 cm) of the edge. Iron this fold and the entire strap.

11 Pin 1 inch (2.5 cm) of one end of the strap to the inside of the border piece on the bag, over-lapping the side seam. Using thread of a matching color, sew a small square of running stitches to secure the end. Finish with three little stitches. Attach the other end to the other side of the bag.

Hand Quilting

A quilt is made up of three layers — a patchwork block, filling (batting or some other stuffing) and a fabric backing. Together these layers are called the quilt sandwich. The sandwich shown here uses a 16-square patchwork block.

You will need:

- Colored quilting thread
- A large fabric square
- Batting
- A sewn patchwork block
- Thimble

If the thimble that comes with this book doesn't fit, buy one in a fabric store or borrow one from a friend.

Making a Quilt Sandwich

1 Lay a large fabric square on a table, bright-side down. This will be your backing. Then lay the square of batting on top, matching the edges at one corner. Hold it in place with a few pins, and then cut away the backing so the backing square is roughly 1 inch (2.5 cm) wider than the batting on two sides.

You might need to do a little fussing with the batting first, to make it square.

2 Move the batting a little so it's in the middle of the backing square. Then take your patchwork block and center it bright-side up on the batting. Hold the layers together with a few pins.

3 Sew all three layers of the quilt sandwich together with very long running stitches through the centers of the squares: four rows up and down and then four rows across.

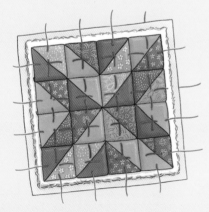

These long running stitches are called basting stitches. You'll pull them out later, so don't bother with knots.

Quilting Your Sandwich

Quilters have many sneaky ways to help them make very small stitches and hide their knots when starting and stopping. Our way is not so sneaky, but it's great for beginners.

1 Study your design and plan where you will quilt. Decide which lines need a long thread and which can be done with a shorter one. See if you can start all your quilting at the edge of your block or if you'll have to start and stop in the middle of the patchwork.

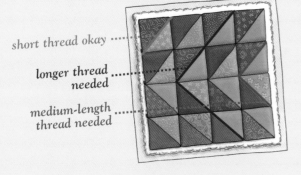

short thread okay ·······
longer thread ·······
    needed
medium-length ·······
   thread needed

We recommend quilting along the diagonal lines because it really sets off the triangles. You can also quilt along the seams if you want an even more quilted look.

2 Put the thimble on your right hand like this. It'll save your finger from turning into a pincushion! (Lefties should use the opposite hand for all of these steps.)

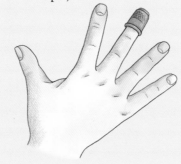

3 Thread the needle with a double strand of colored quilting thread and knot the end. Start at the edge of your block and sew tiny running stitches along one of the lines, going through the block, the batting and the backing. When the line ends, finish with three little stitches on the edge of the block. Then start on another line. Pick one that's the right length for your remaining thread.

Tip: If you have to start in the middle of the patchwork block, push your needle up from the bottom so the knot won't be on the top. To finish, pull the thread through to the bottom and sew three little stitches.

To quilt on the red line, we started and stopped in the middle of the patchwork block.

4 Continue quilting like this until you've quilted along all of the lines.

5 When you've finished quilting, pull out the basting stitches. Then trim off the edges of the batting and backing that stick out beyond the patchwork block.

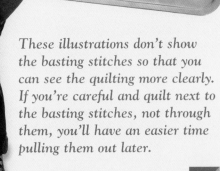

These illustrations don't show the basting stitches so that you can see the quilting more clearly. If you're careful and quilt next to the basting stitches, not through them, you'll have an easier time pulling them out later.

Adding a Binding

If you're making a quilted project — the table mat or the potholder — you'll add a binding to finish the edges.

1 Choose a long fabric strip to use as your binding. Mark a seam line on the wrong side, along one long edge (see page 12). Fold in, bright-sides out, the other long side and one of the short ends about 1/4 inch (0.6 cm). Use the pressing tool to crease the two folds.

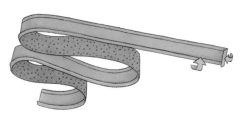

2 Place the short folded end of the binding in the middle of an edge on your quilt sandwich. Pin the binding around the sandwich, bright-sides together, along the seam lines. Sew along the seam line using a running stitch, removing the pins as you go. Be sure to sew all the way through the backing.

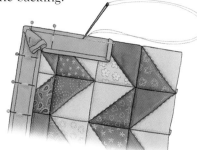

When you get to a corner, ease the binding around so it lays as flat as possible. Look at the illustration to see how we did it.

3 Keep sewing until you complete the last corner. Before you finish, cut off the end of the binding so it overlaps the beginning by 1/2 inch (1.25 cm).

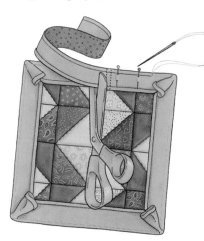

Tip: **Your binding will be smoother when the edge of the quilt sandwich is even, so don't forget to trim off excess batting and backing before you start.**

4 Overlap the beginning of the binding with the end you're sewing now and continue sewing until you run out of binding, stitching through both layers of binding and the quilt sandwich. End with three little stitches.

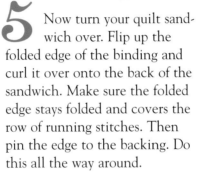

5 Now turn your quilt sandwich over. Flip up the folded edge of the binding and curl it over onto the back of the sandwich. Make sure the folded edge stays folded and covers the row of running stitches. Then pin the edge to the backing. Do this all the way around.

6 Using colored thread that matches the backing, sew the binding down with small hem stitches (see page 16). Hide your starting knot under the folded edge of the binding and don't sew through the patchwork block. Use extra stitches to firmly secure the corners and the overlapping ends. Finish with three little stitches.

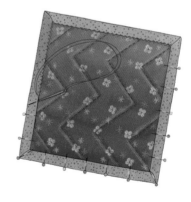

Potholder

A potholder is a red-hot project for first-time quilters. With only nine squares in the patchwork block, the quilting is quick and easy. And when you're done, you can bake some cookies.

You will need:

- A sewn 9-square patchwork block
- A large fabric square
- A long fabric strip
- Squares cut from an old towel. The toweling should be 1/2 inch thick, so you may need more than one layer. Be sure to ask before cutting up a towel!

1 Start by making a quilt sandwich (see page 52). Instead of batting, use one or two squares of toweling that are roughly 1 inch (2.5 cm) wider than your patchwork block in both directions.

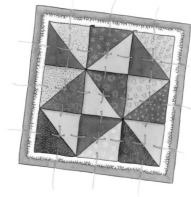

2 Follow the steps on pages 54–55 to quilt the sandwich. It might be hard to hold several running stitches on the needle and to keep them small. You may need to pull the needle all the way through for each stitch.

3 When the quilting is done, follow the steps on pages 56–57 to add a binding. Then iron your finished potholder using a cotton/steam setting.

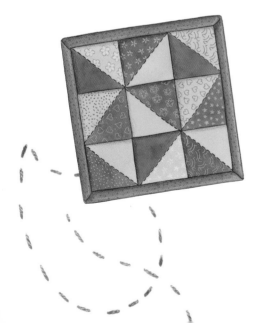

Some 9-Square Designs

There are plenty of 9-square designs you can create by playing around with your design cards. Try starting with one of the 4-square designs on pages 20–23 and then adding five squares along two adjoining sides.

Or use one of these designs.

Table Mat

This mat makes a great handmade gift, perfect for a bedside table or the center of a dinner table. The one shown here uses a 16-square patchwork block, which is a good fit for the piece of batting we've included.

You will need:

- A sewn 16-square patchwork block
- Batting
- A large fabric square
- A long fabric strip

1 Start by making a quilt sandwich and quilting it (see pages 52–55).

2 When the quilting is done, follow the steps on pages 56–57 to add a binding.

3 Iron your finished table mat using a cotton/steam setting.

Triangle Squares from Scratch

Don't stop quilting just because you've used all your triangle squares! Here's how to make more 3-inch (7.5-cm) triangle squares — just like the ones that come with the book — from your own fabric. If you want to make other sizes, see the box on page 63.

You will need:

- 4-inch (10-cm) squares of fabric in two different colors. Two squares of different colors will make two multi-colored triangle squares.

- A ballpoint pen or pencil

- Seam allowance measure

- Scrap paper

1 Divide your squares into two piles — one for each color. Put a piece of scrap paper on the table and then put a square from the first pile, bright-side down, on the paper.

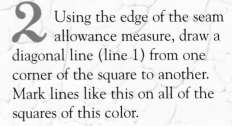

2 Using the edge of the seam allowance measure, draw a diagonal line (line 1) from one corner of the square to another. Mark lines like this on all of the squares of this color.

3 Line up the measure so the purple seam line is running along the line you just drew (line 1). Now mark another line (line 2) along the edge of the ruler.

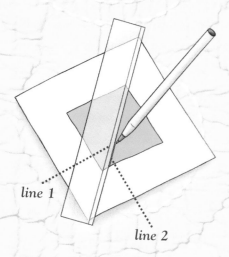

line 1

line 2

4 Flip the measure over to mark another line (line 3) in the same way, this time on the other side of line 1. Mark lines 2 and 3 on all of the squares of this color.

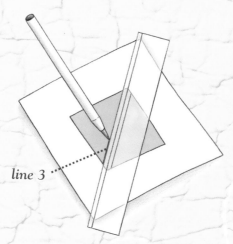

line 3

5 Lay each marked square on top of a square of the other color, bright-sides together. Sew the squares together, using running stitches, along the outside lines (lines 2 and 3).

If you think you might get these three lines mixed up, you can use ballpoint pens in two colors — one color for line 1 and a second color for lines 2 and 3.

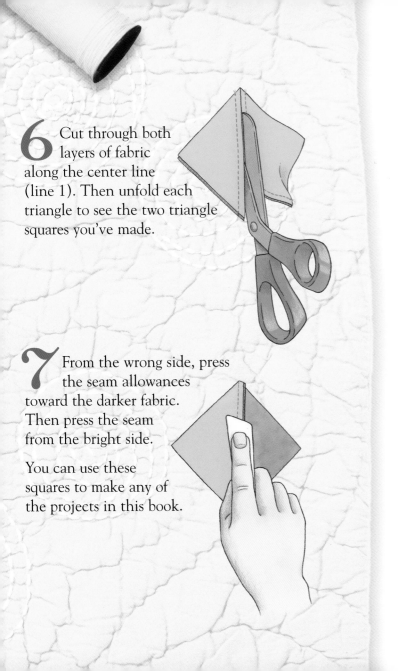

6 Cut through both layers of fabric along the center line (line 1). Then unfold each triangle to see the two triangle squares you've made.

7 From the wrong side, press the seam allowances toward the darker fabric. Then press the seam from the bright side.

You can use these squares to make any of the projects in this book.

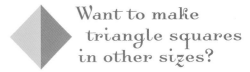

Want to make triangle squares in other sizes?

Just take the size square you want to end up with and add 1 inch (2.5 cm) to that measurement. Cut your squares to that size, and you'll create triangle squares in the right size for your project.

For finished triangle squares measuring:	*Start with solid squares measuring:*
3 inches	4 inches
3 ½ inches	4 ½ inches
4 inches	5 inches
4 ½ inches	5 ½ inches
5 inches	6 inches
5 ½ inches	6 ½ inches
6 inches	7 inches
7.5 cm	10 cm
9 cm	11.5 cm
10 cm	12.5 cm
11.5 cm	14 cm
12.5 cm	15 cm
14 cm	16.5 cm
15 cm	17.5 cm

inches

centimeters

KLUTZ.com OPEN 24 HOURS
Come on in!

Can't get enough? Here are some simple ways to keep the Klutz coming.

Order more of the supplies that came with this book at **klutz.com**. It's quick, it's easy and, seriously, where else are you going to find this exact stuff?

Get your hands on a copy of The Klutz Catalog. To request a free copy of our completely compelling mail order catalog, go to **klutz.com/catalog**.

Become a Klutz Insider and get e-mail about new releases, special offers, contests, games, goofiness and who-knows-what-all. If you're a grown-up who wants to receive e-mail from Klutz, head to **klutz.com/certified**.

If any of this sounds good to you, but you don't feel like going on-line right now, just give us a call at 1-800-737-4123. We'd love to hear from you.

Other Great Books from Klutz

Knitting	Friendship Bracelets
Simple Embroidery	Dial With Style™
Twirled Paper	Room Lanterns
Handmade Cards	Picture Bracelets
Velvet Art	Charm Watch
Window Art	Nail Art

Many thanks to everyone

Art Direction: Kate Paddock, Jill Turney

Design: Jamison Spittler Design

Cover and Box: Anne Schultz

Dry Clean Only: Maria Seamans, Jina Choi

Fabric Design: Liz Hutnick

Quilting Bee: Alice Tucker, April Keller-MacLeod, Barb Magnus, Becki Johnson, Deborah Shannahan, Louise Bell, Melissa Brozoski, Patty Morris, Rachelle Adams, Theresa Hutnick

Extra Helpful: Marilyn Green, Betty Lowman, April Keller-MacLeod

Design Cards and Diagrams: Lisa Devenish

Photography: Peter Fox, Joseph Quever, Matt Farruggio

Technical Illustration: Barbara Ball

Technical Writing: Louise Bell

Calligraphy: Rosemary Woods

Stitch Witch: Patty Morris

Ps and Qs: Jen Mills

Models: Zuri Ray-Alladice, Soumya Srinagesh, Shannon Harney, Roxanne Pinto, Roxana Moussa, Rose-Emilie Frouin, Nicole van den Haak, Molly Kawahata, Mira Bertsch, Megan Smith, Madeleine Ferguson, Kaela Fox, Julie Zhu, Jessie Ju, Hilary Brennan-Marquez, Hana Raftery, Emily Lon, Emily Flaxman, Elissa Chandler, Danya Taymor, Christina Brenton, Allison Heinrich, Alexis Medina, Alexandra Snell, Alex Stikeleather

Photo Shoot Wrangler: Megan Smith

Supporting Design: Efrat Rafaeli, Teresa Roberts, Corie Thompson

Pins and Needling: John Cassidy